When My Pet Is Sick

Staying Healthy

Here is my pet.

My pet is a budgie.

My budgie needs
a clean cage.

My budgie needs
clean water.

Here is my pet.

My pet is a guinea pig.

My guinea pig
needs clean water.

My guinea pig
goes in here.

Here is my pet dog.

My dog needs
clean water.

My dog needs
dog food.

I will take my pet

to the vet, when it is sick.

The vet will listen.

The vet will look.

The vet will touch.

I love my pet!